TROUBLE & BEAUTY

WOMEN ENCOUNTER CATHOLIC SOCIAL TEACHING

by

Maria Riley, OP
Nancy Sylvester, IHM

A Publication of

Center of Concern ■ Leadership Conference of Women Religious ■ NETWORK

We are grateful to Carolyn McDade for her gracious permission to use her song "Trouble and Beauty" in the title and context of this book.

We are also grateful for the open copyright of *Ecumenical Decade 1988-1998: Churches in Solidarity with Women: Prayers and Poems, Songs and Stories*, World Council of Church Publications; *Woman's Song*, National Sisters Vocation Conference; and *The Best of Struggles: Multicultural Women's Project in Music*, Womancenter at Plainville, MA.

ISBN – 0-934255-10-5

To order copies contact: Center of Concern
3700 13th Street, N.E.
Washington, DC 20017
Phone: 202 635-2757
FAX: 202 832-9494

Bulk Prices Available

Design: Page Designs Unlimited

Art Work: Thorina Rose

360
R45

DEDICATION

*For all the women and men—past and present—at
the Center of Concern, Leadership Conference of Women Religious
and NETWORK whose laughter and love
have enabled us to see that far wandering star and who keep
calling us on to a future of justice and peace.*

CONTENTS

PREFACE

Catholic social teaching has been and continues to be important to the life of the three organizations that collaborated on the publication of *Trouble and Beauty: Women Encounter Catholic Social Teaching*. In the 25 years since the close of Vatican Council II, a return to the social teachings of the Church has been a basic and radical source of renewal. These teachings have given inspiration to individuals and groups as well as direction to justice agendas. They have been the founding principles for action, but in many instances have not been assimilated into daily life. The documents dealing with the very life of the human family call out for implementation in this present era as never before.

Responding to this call, in June of 1990, Maria Riley, OP of the Center of Concern and Nancy Sylvester, IHM of NETWORK co-presented a workshop at the *RERUM NOVARUM* Conference, coordinated by the Eighth Day Center in Chicago. Margaret Nulty, SC of the Leadership Conference of Women Religious, who attended the Conference, felt that the content and approach of their workshop had a uniqueness and value which should be shared with a larger audience. The three women met

to discuss possibilities and the idea was born for the book, *Trouble and Beauty: Women Encounter Catholic Social Teaching*.

The 100th Anniversary of the writing of *Rerum Novarum* not only offers us the continuing challenge to learn more about the Church's social teaching, but also provides an opportunity to examine the content and evolution of Catholic social thought from a feminist perspective. In one sense, the essential equality of women and men—the defining characteristic of feminism—undergirds Church teaching. But on the other hand, this equality is often contradicted by the patriarchal mind-set which prevails. The process of analysis and reflection within this text can assist all who use it to probe the relationship of feminism and Catholic social thought. The six chapters offer creative ways to apply insights from women's experience to the significant issues being faced today in our Church and world.

Women's contribution to the justice and peace agenda has been informed and shaped by the principles of Catholic social thought and needs to play an essential part in this Anniversary celebration.

From beginning to end, the publishing of this book has been one of collaboration among the three organizations— The Center of Concern, the Leadership Conference of Women Religious, and NETWORK. The human and material resources of all three organizations have been utilized with the special talents and insights of Maria and Nancy providing the written text. The work could not have been brought to completion, however, without the assistance of Judy Mladineo, Peter Ellsworth, Tracy Kaufman, Elise Garcia, Mary Jo Klick, and Margaret Nulty, SC as well as readers Carol Coston, OP,

Amata Miller, IHM, and James Hug, SJ. To all we are deeply grateful.

As each reader will discover, the content of this publication is designed to engage you in a process of reflection and discussion. Although this dialogue between feminism and Catholic social thought will continue for some years to come, we offer this book to you as our contribution to the 1991 celebration of 100 years of Catholic social teaching. It is our hope that the work you do through this process will empower you to enter into any discussions around Catholic social thought with deeper understanding and commitment to the work of social transformation to which both feminism and Catholic social thought call us. That call is not just for this year but until the "reign of God" is more deeply realized in our Church and world.

Janet Roesener, CSJ
Leadership Conference of Women Religious
January 1991

Introduction

"By these laboring wings we have come thus far
to this place in the wind where we see
trouble and beauty
we see trouble, we see beauty
and that far wandering star still calls us on.[1]

Trouble and beauty. As women working for justice, we believe the words of this song capture a spirit in which to celebrate and critique the tradition of Catholic social teaching.

Many of us find the best of our Catholic heritage reflected in this body of teaching. Rooted in the prophetic tradition of the Hebrew prophets and Jesus, the teachings denounce injustices and announce a new way of being in the world.

We can affirm the denunciations and cry out with the official Church against the exploitation of workers, growing economic inequalities, misuse of our limited resources, denial of basic human rights and the sinful structures of society.

We cry out, denounce and grieve and know that those who suffer from such injustices are disproportionately women and people of color.

We can affirm the prophetic task of announcing a new way of being in the world. The new possibilities excite us and confirm our own experience that perhaps there is another way of doing things.

The principles and values embodied in the teachings touch deeply into our experience as women: The dignity of the human person; the rights of the family and the essential importance of community to authentic human development; the need for economic justice; the understanding of global solidarity linked to an option for the poor and the importance of the common good; the right to participate in decisions that affect our lives; the belief that charity and justice are intertwined; and the need to be part of the community of creation and to promote peace.

We can celebrate the beauty of this tradition—a tradition that has motivated so many of us to become involved in ministry—working for justice in a variety of ways by addressing such issues as homelessness, hunger and illiteracy.

And yet, as we work for justice, trying to integrate the principles and values offered by the teachings into our lives, we come up against a very troublesome reality: The more we understand the dignity of the human person and the need for community based on relationships of mutuality, and the more we experience the process of empowering others to participate in decision-making, the more we seek to integrate these learnings into every aspect of our lives—familial, societal and ecclesial. And in so doing, we come up against barriers—barriers constructed by traditional concepts of woman, of woman's role, of family, of work, of power, of religion.

These barriers protect an ideology that prevents women from being heard or understood in the Church and from having an impact on the Church's analysis of injustice. The Church's practices create a false separation between the work of transforming structures of injustice in the economic and political spheres and the work of transforming structures of injustice in the ecclesial and familial arenas.

These barriers are troubling because they stop us and force us to look at the beauty of Catholic social teaching from a perspective filled with questions. We question an understanding of woman and family that is formulated without women's experience and participation. We are skeptical about how the words "man" and "mankind" are used and question whether the rights attributed to the human person are applied equally to men and women.

Finally, our questioning leaves us deeply troubled with the awareness and understanding that the new way of being, announced by the teachings, cannot become a reality unless the richness of women's experience and creative energy is incorporated.

"Being troubled" can lead to "causing trouble."

Causing trouble, however, can be very constructive when it is rooted in the beauty of the tradition.

Trouble and Beauty: Women Encounter Catholic Social Teaching was created to engage women and men in a three-fold task.

First, to celebrate the beauty of the social justice tradition and to expand upon it by naming the ways women have already begun changing structures.

We can celebrate the beauty of this tradition— a tradition that has motivated so many of us to become involved in ministry— working for justice in a variety of ways by addressing such issues as homelessness, hunger and illiteracy.

Second, to identify the trouble. We want to break down the barriers of fear and ideology that prevent women from being heard or understood. We want to critique Catholic social teaching from our perspective—from the perspective of women, a feminist perspective—so that a more authentic understanding of women can emerge because it is shaped by women and by our experiences.

Third, to explore how women's experiences can enlarge and deepen Catholic social teaching—just as Catholic social teaching can also strengthen and enrich the feminist movement.

Our study examines six areas: An overview of Catholic social teaching and feminism; work and family; the dignity of the human person; peace; economic development and political participation; and women as Church-in-action for justice and peace. Each session has two movements:

1) Your personal preparation by reading the introduction to each session, the excerpts of Catholic social teaching and the reflection questions;

2) Group discussion on the insights and ideas you have gained and your creative input into the continuing evolution of Catholic social thought as it encounters women's new consciousness of ourselves—this "sign of our time."

We have developed this process to facilitate both your personal reflection and the group's sharing of its wisdom.

Trouble and Beauty is a process book. It does not pretend to be a fully developed work regarding either Catholic social teaching or feminist theory. But it does reflect much study, reflection and living in these areas by the authors.

As we pondered a title for the book we both reflected on our years of experience as women working within the Church in the area of social justice. Through these many years, we have often felt enriched by the social justice tradition of the Church—but also troubled by the official Church's view of women.

We felt drawn in this search to a song written by Carolyn McDade entitled, "Trouble and Beauty." In her introduction to the song, Carolyn writes how she was inspired by the effortless flight of a butterfly which appeared to be in such contrast to "the laboring wings which have brought me and my friends thus far, to this place in the wind where we have achieved vision enough to understand and daring enough to live from that understanding."

Carolyn further noted:

What is revealed is a world of trouble and beauty—the uprising from suffering and the spirited grace of people rejecting

Our questioning leaves us deeply troubled with the awareness and understanding that the new way of being, announced by the teachings, cannot become a reality unless the richness of women's experience and creative energy is incorporated.

oppression—the beauty of those who gather wild flowers and poems for their martyrs, who dance before they die, who dare to love, troubling the powerful and all that maintains domination—those who create at risk a different way— fresh, limber, just—a far wandering star call us on.

And so we invite you to engage with us in encountering Catholic social teaching from a feminist perspective in the spirit of trouble and beauty.

We suggest that at the beginning of each session you sing the song, "Trouble and Beauty," and prayerfully reflect on the two quotations that begin each session. We hope the dialogue begun in the pages of this book will assist us in "risking a different way"—in finding that far wandering star that calls us on.

*By this rainbow, my friends,
   we have come thus far
to this place in our lives where we live
trouble and beauty
we live trouble, we live beauty
and that far wandering star still
   calls us on.*

---

1 *Carolyn McDade, "Trouble and Beauty," in This Tough Spun Web, (Plainville, MA: Womancenter at Plainville), p. 3.*

2 *Carolyn McDade, "Introduction, 'Trouble and Beauty,' " in This Tough Spun Web, p.2.*

Maria Riley, OP—Center of Concern
Nancy Sylvester, IHM—NETWORK
January 1991

TROUBLE AND BEAUTY

By Carolyn McDade

Let it bend — give it wings

© 1984 Surtsey Publishing
Words + Music by Carolyn McDade

By these la-bor-ing wings we have come thus far — to this place in the wind where we see trou-ble and beauty we see trouble we see beau-ty and that far wandering star still calls us on — . It's the star will rise and shine — rise — and shine — It will rise and shine when earth's peo-ple all are free — It calls to you — It calls to me — Keep these la-bor-ing wings 'til all are free _____

Note: Music and tape of "Trouble and Beauty" are available from Womancenter at Plainville, 76 Everett Skinner Road, Plainville, MA 02762. Phone: (617) 699-7167

By these laboring wings we have
come thus far
to this place in the wind
where we see
trouble and beauty
and that far wandering star still
calls us on

chorus:
It's the star will rise and shine
rise and shine
It will rise and shine when earth's
people all are free
It calls to you—it calls to me
Keep your laboring wings till all are free

By this breath conspired we have
come thus far
to this place in our song where we sing
trouble and beauty
we sing trouble, we sing beauty
and that far wandering star still
calls us on

By these hearts of rage we have
come thus far
to this place in our love
where we dare
trouble and beauty
we dare trouble, we dare beauty
and that far wandering star still
calls us on

By this rainbow, my friends, we have
come thus far
to this place in our lives where we live
trouble and beauty
we live trouble, we live beauty
and that far wandering star still
calls us on

And this rainbow is you,
this rainbow is me
Keep this rainbow, my friends,
till all are free

PROCESS AND RESOURCES

Process Suggestions

For the Facilitator:

◆ Gather a group of women and men who are interested in discussing feminism and Catholic social teaching.

◆ During the first meeting take some time for the participants to introduce themselves and share some of their hopes and expectations of the process.

◆ Begin each session by singing "Trouble and Beauty" and spending some time reflecting on the opening quotes.

◆ Invite each of the participants to share her/his reflections on the introductory material and the quotes from Catholic social teaching.

◆ Spend the major portion of the time developing the final questions of each session. This is the arena for creatively expanding the horizons of feminism and Catholic social thought.

◆ Conclude each session with a brief evaluation of the group process and the details of the next session—when, where, and preparation.

◆ Each session needs about one and a half to two hours.

For the Participants:

◆ Prepare for each session by studying the introductory material and the quotes from Catholic social teaching. Spend some time on personal reflection. Space for note taking is provided.

Resources and Texts Used in
Quoting and Interpreting Catholic Social Teaching

A Call to Build Society on Earth: The Catholic Social Justice Tradition. Washington, DC: NETWORK, A National Catholic Social Justice Lobby. 1989.

Baum, Gregory and Robert Ellsberg, eds. *The Logic of Solidarity.* Maryknoll, New York: Orbis Books. 1989.

Byers, David, ed. *Justice in the Marketplace.* Washington, DC: United States Catholic Conference. 1985.

Gremillion, Joseph. *The Gospel of Peace and Justice.* Maryknoll, New York: Orbis Books. 1975.

Henriot, Peter, Edward P. DeBerri and Michael Schultheis. *Catholic Social Teaching: Our Best Kept Secret.* rev.ed. Maryknoll, New York: Orbis Books. 1987.

John Paul II. "On Human Work." *Origins.* 11:15 (September 24, 1981).

John Paul II. "The Social Concerns of the Church." *Origins.* 17:38 (March 3, 1988).

Leo XIII. "The Condition of Labor." Washington, DC: United States Catholic Conference. 1942.

O'Brien, David and Thomas A. Shannon, eds. *Renewing the Earth.* Garden City, New York: Image Books. 1977.

Pius XI. "On Reconstructing the Social Order." Washington, DC: United States Catholic Conference. 1942.

Note on Language in Quotes

We have made the decision not to change to inclusive language when quoting the Standard English translations of the Catholic social documents.

Catholic Social Teaching
and Feminism Meet

"The joys and the hopes, the griefs and the anxieties
for the men of this age, especially those who are poor or
in any way afflicted, these too are the joys and hopes, the griefs and
anxieties of the followers of Christ.

The Church in the Modern World [#1]

"We look forward to the future in faith and hope, working for the day
when we and all our sisters no longer have to fit a stereotype, but are free
to use all our gifts and to share in all the benefits of human life and work.
We look forward to the age of peace, when violence is banished, both
women and men are able to love and to be loved and the work and wealth
of our world is justly shared.

Women's Creed[1]

The Spirit of our God is upon me; anointing me and sending me to bring glad tidings to the poor, to proclaim liberty to captives, recovery of sight to the blind and release to prisoners. To announce a year of favor from our God.

Luke, 4:18

When Jesus spoke those words in the temple at Nazareth, he identified himself within the tradition of the great Hebrew prophets whose two-fold task was to denounce injustice and to announce a new way of being in the world.

Jesus denounced the danger of riches, the hypocrisy of the Scribes and Pharisees, those who never give food to the hungry or welcome the stranger or visit the sick or imprisoned, those who hoard or lay heavy burdens on others.

And Jesus announced new possibilities, new ways of relating, new understandings of power that challenged some of the basic assumptions of his culture: The last shall be first. The master is the servant. The poor shall inherit the earth. Women and men are equal. Love outweighs law. All goods should be shared in common.

Understanding Catholic Social Teaching

The social justice teachings of the Church are rooted in the life of Jesus and in this prophetic tradition. During the early Church, these teachings were carried on in the writings and sermons of the ordained leaders known as the "Fathers of the Church." Beginning in 1891, the official Church began a systematic presentation of this body of thought which today we refer to as Catholic social teaching.

At the level of universal teaching are the papal encyclicals and the synod statements. Others areas of official Catholic social thought are found in a variety of Vatican Congregation and Commission teachings. In addition, episcopal conferences in different nations have issued their own documents applying universal principles to their historical realities.

In the United States, the Bishops' most recent pastoral letters on racism (*Brothers and Sisters to Us All: A Pastoral Letter on Racism, 1979*), peace (*The Challenge of Peace: God's Promise and Our Response, 1983*), economic justice (*Economic Justice for All: Catholic Social Teaching and the U.S. Economy, 1986*) and mission (*To the Ends of the Earth, 1986*) reflect this application of the universal teachings to the specific situations confronting the United States.

The focus of this publication is on the body of universal teaching, that is, on the major social justice encyclicals and synod statements. This body of teaching has evolved through the years, shaped by the social, economic, political and cultural realities of the times. And yet, through the times, the teachings consistently denounce certain injustices and announce key values that illuminate the beauty of the tradition and challenge us to work for justice.

Following is a brief synopsis of these documents which serve as the context for the sessions in the book. Both the Latin and English titles are used, but in the introductory section of each session only the English titles appear.

The social justice teachings of the Church are rooted in the life of Jesus and in the prophetic tradition.

RERUM NOVARUM (*The Condition of Labor*) was written in 1891 be Leo XIII. This is the first encyclical of the modern period. One hundred years ago, the Church denounced the inhuman working conditions brought about by the Industrial Revolution. The just and equitable relationship among workers, productive property and the role of the state were seen as key in Catholic social thought. A just society was announced, one which affirms the dignity of work, the right to private property and the right to form and join professional associations such as labor unions.

QUADRAGESIMO ANNO (*The Reconstruction of the Social Order*) was issued by Pius XI in 1931, 40 years after *Rerum Novarum*. Written in the midst of a world-wide depression, the statement denounces the growing concentration of wealth and power in the socio-economic realm. It develops the principle of "subsidiarity," a centerpiece of Catholic social teaching, which states that decisions should take place at the level closest to those involved. It calls for a reconstruction of the social order based on the social responsibilities of private property and the rights to a job, a just wage and membership in a labor union.

MATER ET MAGISTRA (*Christianity and Social Progress*) was issued by John XXIII in 1961. This document signifies a turning point in the Church's understanding that the social questions—a phrase used to denote changes associated with the Industrial Revolution regarding work, urbanization and class divisions—have become worldwide. This document adopts an international perspective, denouncing the unequal distribution of the world's wealth and resources. Special concern is given to the plight of farmers and farm workers. A positive role for government is announced. Governments must play a major role, even take the initiative, if economic justice is to be achieved.

PACEM IN TERRIS (*Peace on Earth*) was written by John XXIII in 1963. Although its main focus is the attainment of peace, this encyclical includes a comprehensive charter of human rights. It denounces the increasing arms race and the inability of national governments to promote the international common good. Understanding that the roots of war are often economic in nature, the encyclical not only addresses a person's economic duties but also emphasizes a person's economic rights. These rights include the opportunity to work without coercion, to enjoy safe working conditions, to participate in the economic process to the full extent of one's abilities, to receive just recompense for work and to own private property. It announces that peace can be achieved if it is based on an economic and political order that respects the rights of the individual—economic and political—and is rooted in human dignity. Such an order, the encyclical states, can become the basis for a spirit of international harmony.

GAUDIUM ET SPES (*The Church in the Modern World*) was issued by the College of Bishops in 1965 during the

Second Vatican Council. This is a watershed document in terms of defining the role of the Church *vis a vis* the world. This document declares that the Church is called to be an agent of transformation. It states that the Church is in a learning posture and must try to read "the signs of the times" so that it can denounce the injustices in the world and contribute to announcing new possibilities. It makes the human person central to the theological and philosophical thinking of the church. And it recognizes the social nature of the person. Community is seen as integral to the authentic self-definition of every person. This emphasis on the social nature of the person has implications not only for individual development but also for the urbanization of economic life. Even the right to private property is linked to the universal purpose of all of creation. This document also links the quest for peace with justice and discusses the development of nations.

POPULORUM PROGRESSIO *(The Development of Peoples)* was written by Paul VI in 1967. This encyclical focuses on the widening gap between the rich and poor nations and denounces the increasing concentration of wealth in the world. Serious questions are raised about the justice of existing governmental and private economic structures. The encyclical states that the government has the right to expropriate those pieces of private property which are ill-used, underused or cause hardship for the people or the nation. A new sense of global solidarity is urged which will shape new economic structures. The encyclical announces that "development is the new name for peace."

OCTOGESIMA ADVENIENS *(A Call to Action)* was written by Paul VI in 1971 commemorating the 80th anniversary of *Rerum Novarum*. This statement makes action in the political arena an integral part of being a Christian. It addresses a new sense of Christian responsibility for social reform. Although it warns against the ambiguities in every social ideology, it recognizes that the urgency of the problems facing us demands Christians to participate in the social and political processes of their countries. In addressing the new set of problems stemming from urbanization it draws specific attention to the revitalization of neighborhoods and the effects of technology on the environment. It challenges the increasing domination of humans over nature and urges a reexamination of the traditional concept of stewardship.

JUSTICE IN THE WORLD is the 1971 statement of the Synod of Bishops. This is a strong document which emphasizes the structures of injustice and the need for structural change which incorporates principles of justice. It suggests that part of the Gospel mandate is to stand with the poor and oppressed. It defines justice as being at the core of the mission of the Church: "Action in pursuit of justice and participation in the transformation of the world are constitutive elements in the Church's mission of preaching the Gospel." The document also proposes that the principles of justice be applied to the practice of justice in the internal life of the Church.

EVANGELII NUNTIANDI (*Evangelization in the Modern World*) was written by Paul VI in 1975. In expressing a contemporary theology of evangelization, this statement reaffirms the link between proclaiming the Gospel and struggling for social justice. It calls for a transformation of culture and announces that Christians must have a special concern for the poor and "eliminate the social consequences of sin which are translated into unjust social and political structures."

REDEMPTOR HOMINIS (*Redemption and the Dignity of the Human Race*) was the first encyclical written by John Paul II in 1979. This statement denounces the consumer mentality, the greed of rich countries and unjust social situations that threaten humanity and the environment. It announces the need for a major overhaul of economic structures— one which is rooted in a sense of solidarity.

LABOREM EXERCENS (*On Human Work*) written in 1981, 90 years after *Rerum Novarum*, is John Paul IIs treatise on the centrality of work to the whole social question. A key teaching in the encyclical is that the value of work comes from the value of the worker and not the product. It states that labor must be given priority over capital. In fact, work is seen as a creative expression of the human person and a way of participating directly in the act of creation. The encyclical denounces exploitative working conditions and any economic system that reduces work or the worker to a mere instrument.

SOLLICITUDO REI SOCIALIS (*The Social Concerns of the Church*) was written by John Paul II in 1987. This encyclical addresses the state of global development. It denounces the maldistribution of wealth and resources and the ongoing arms trade and "superdevelopment" which benefits the very few at the expense of the many poor. It denounces both liberal capitalism of the West and Marxist collectivism of the East. It names the obstacles hindering development as "structures of sin." It announces a world where interdependence is transformed into solidarity, based upon the principle that the goods of creation are meant for all. Solidarity is extended to the oppressed and we are challenged to develop the political will to act in common.

Understanding Feminism

With the Second Vatican Council, the Church embraced the necessity of "reading the signs of the times" as its mode of social discernment. This biblical theme (Matt. 16:1-4) rests in the "basic Christian belief that God continues to speak in and through human history":

The Church looks to the world and discovers there God's presence. Signs both reveal God's presence in the world and manifest God's designs for the world. Implicit in this truth is that theology must go beyond the purely deductive and speculative. History ceases to be the mere context for the application of binding principles, which are derived uniquely from speculative and philosophical reasoning. It becomes the place of on-going revelation.[2]

The rise of women's consciousne[ss] concerning their own dignity over the last 25 years is one of the most far-reaching "signs of our times." It is God's revelatio[n] breaking through history....

The rise of women's consciousness concerning their own dignity over the last 25 years is one of the most far-reaching "signs of our times." It is God's revelation breaking through history, challenging the time-honored human theory that men, by virtue of being male, deserve the right to govern and control all dimensions of society and that women should be subordinate to them. As the theologian Beverly Harrison observes, " 'Woman-spirit rising' is a global phenomenon in our time. Everywhere women are on the move. What is coming into view now, for the first time, on a world-wide scale, is the incredible collective power of women so that anyone who has eyes to see can glimpse the power and strength of women's full humanity."[3]

Women are beginning to change the social landscape. For example, for the past two decades women have been entering the labor market at a rate of more than 1.2 million a year. By 1989, women represented 45% of all the working people in the United States and the proportion is continuing to rise.[4] This reality is changing patterns of relationships between women and men, creating new patterns of family life, adjusting the economic equation between women and men, diminishing the pool of women available for traditional volunteer work and enlarging women's expectations for themselves.

These realities demand not only new social attitudes and policies, they also demand new social structures. They are making new claims on traditional social systems—governments, schools, families, Churches, social services and businesses.[5] They have

also opened new questions for social ethics as the profound but subtle shift of social institutions, particularly the institutions of work and family, has become evident. It is around these new questions that feminism and Catholic social thought meet.

This book is about that meeting—the "Trouble and Beauty" of the encounter.

FEMINISM AS MOVEMENT AND THEORY:

Feminism is both a movement and a social theory. As a movement, its goal is the empowerment of women for the transformation of social and religious structures beyond patriarchy—that model of social organization that assures men, predominately white men, have control and dominant power within social and religious structures. As a social theory, feminism is a mode of analysis based on women's experience within patriarchal structures and a vision of future societies that are built on mutuality and cooperation rather than on domination and competition.[6]

Feminist analysis, using gender as the critical lens to examine patriarchy, identifies domination as the central issue. Domination takes many forms, men over women, the white race over all others, the rich over the poor and humans over all other creatures. The key feminist insight, "the personal is political," reveals the continuity and consistency of the pattern of domination in personal relationships as well as in social and religious structures. It also offers a clue to transformation: As women begin to change personally, the social structures will be affected and vice-versa.

Feminism both as a movement and as a social theory is not objective, nor does it seek to be. It clearly advocates the empowerment of women and challenges other social theories that claim to be objective. A social theory or ethic that does not address the power equation between women and men, in fact, supports and advocates patriarchal social systems. In directly advocating the empowerment of women, feminism is seeking to correct the imbalances of the past and to create a future that is not characterized by domination of one group over another—not only men over women, but also the domination of the Western culture over all others, the white race over all other races and the human over the community of creation.

Furthermore, feminism seeks to transform not only structural but also cultural imbalances. Women and people of distinct racial and cultural backgrounds have not only been denied power, but their distinctive values and gifts have been denied a voice in the culture. The values of nurturance, compassion, equality, diversity and cooperation have been relegated to secondary values in the patriarchal culture which demands hierarchy by its very nature. Once hierarchy is established as the norm, it values control, uniformity, obedience and competition to maintain itself. Feminist social ethics seeks a future that is participative, compassionate, cooperative and which values diversity and creativity. Its vision and hope is for a world characterized by a profound sense of reverence and mutuality among all peoples and for creation—a vision of the reign of God where the "wolf lives with the lamb, the panther lies down with the kid, calf and lion feed together with a little child to lead them" (Is. 11:6).

CATHOLIC SOCIAL THEORY: Catholic social teaching also reflects a social theory. According to John Paul IIs encyclical, *The Social Concerns of the Church*, the development of Catholic social teaching is based on "principles of reflection," "criteria of judgment" and "directives for action." Its method is fundamentally deductive, that is, starting from general principles and applying them to concrete situations. Feminists rightfully ask, Who defines these principles, criteria and directives? From where do they come? Furthermore, feminists question how universally and accurately these principles and criteria reflect human experience, particularly women's experience. Historically, women's voices and experience have not been formative of Catholic social thought.

This absence, of course, is not a new insight. Women's voices and experience have been silent in all authoritative teaching and deliberation in the Church. Moreover, in beginning a discussion between Catholic social teaching and women, it is important to recognize the patriarchy that shapes Catholic social teaching. It can be identified as patriarchal for several reasons: 1) it was written by men, primarily about men; 2) its bias is androcentric, that is, it assumes that man, in this case, white Western man, is normative for the human; and

A social theory or ethic that does not address the power equation between women and men, in fact, supports and advocates patriarchal social systems.

3) when women are included, they are defined from a patriarchal point of view. Feminist analysis reveals this bias and challenges Catholic social teaching to respond to the new realities of the contemporary world.

However, Catholic social teaching can also strengthen, enrich and challenge the feminist movement. Its emphasis on the dignity of the human person, the importance of family, economic justice and political participation enhances women's struggle for empowerment and equality. It also calls on the people of the United States, women and men alike, both to understand the demand of global justice and peace and to work to achieve them. Feminism's understanding of the global dimensions of today's world is both enriched by and enriching to Catholic social teaching[7]

---

[1] *Norma Hardy* Ecumenical Decade 1988-1998: Churches in Solidarity with Women: Prayer and Poems, Songs and Stories *(Geneva, Switzerland: World Council of Churches Publications, 1988), p. 68.*

[2] *Peter J. Henriot, Edward P. DeBerri and Michael J. Schultheis,* Catholic Social Teaching: Our Best Kept Secret, *rev. ed. (Maryknoll, New York: Orbis Books, 1987), p. 18.*

[3] *"The Power of Anger in the Work of Love: Christian Ethics for Women and Other Strangers,"* Union Seminary Quarterly Review, *XXXVI (Supplementary Issue, 1981), p. 44.*

[4] *Janet L. Norwood, "Working Women: Where Have We Been? Where Are We Going?" 1989 Margaret Cuninggim Lecture, Vanderbilt University, Nashville, Tennessee (November 8, 1989), p. 5.*

[5] *Carol S. Robb, "A Framework for Feminist Ethics," in* Women's Consciousness, Women's Conscience *(Minneapolis: Winston Press, 1985), p. 211.*

[6] *For more information on feminism as a social theory, see* Transforming Feminism *by Maria Riley (Kansas City: Sheed and Ward, 1989).*

[7] *We decided not to include a discussion of abortion in this book. Instead we concentrate on the social contexts out of which women make reproductive choices—work, family, development and poverty, peace and war. As these contexts are transformed to accommodate women's needs and experiences in pregnancy, childbirth and family life, we believe the incidence of abortion will decline.*

Reflections

◆ Reflecting on the general introduction and the introduction to Session One, what do I find most exciting? Most challenging? Most disturbing?

◆ What questions do I have regarding the content of Catholic social teaching?

◆ What questions do I have regarding the presentation on feminism?

◆ What insights do I bring to these two areas?

Group Discussion:
Toward an Understanding of Catholic Social Teaching and Feminism

◆ What did you find most interesting or challenging in these sections? What was new to you? What questions did it raise?

◆ What connections do you see between the two social theories? What differences?

Toward a Renewed Understanding of Work and Family

"It must be remembered and affirmed that the family
constitutes one of the most important terms of reference for
shaping the social and ethical order of human work. The teaching of the
Church has always devoted special attention to this question . . . . In fact the
family is simultaneously a community made possible by work and the first
school of work, within the home, for every person.

On Human Labor [#10]

"I am mother
I am sister
I am wife
I am woman
A woman who, from the beginning
has worked to the limits of her capacity
in the paddy field, in plantations and factories;
. . .
I am woman
I am worker
Women, who are nurses, teachers, clerks, typists, working
long hours together with the additional burden of housework.

Anonymous[1]

For the majority of women and men, family and work are the primary contexts of their lives. These contexts are being profoundly affected by the economic, technical and social changes occurring in the United States today. Justice in the work place, both at home and abroad, is under siege as many companies move beyond our shores seeking cheap labor. Workers, particularly women, industrial laborers and minorities, struggle for meaningful jobs, just wages, benefits and social support systems to enable them and their families to survive. What do Catholic social thought and feminism contribute to the debate on the new social issues that these realities create?

The Tradition

Catholic social teaching has consistently addressed the integral relationship of work, economic rights, the well-being of the family and the common good as a central concern. The first papal encyclical, *The Condition of Labor*, was written 100 years ago in response to the negative impact of the Industrial Revolution on the worker and the family. Forty years later, in 1931, Pius XI wrote *The Reconstruction of the Social Order* to address these issues again during the Great Depression. In 1981, John Paul II wrote *On Human Labor* which raises the critical work issues of the contemporary era.

Several key principles shape Catholic social teaching's reflection on work and workers. Among them are the primacy of the worker over capital, the right to employment and the right to a just wage. This wage is often spoken of as a "family wage," or income sufficient to guarantee the economic well-being of the family. Workers should have a safe work place and guaranteed sufficient leisure time for personal well-being and family life. Catholic social thought has always insisted on the workers' right to organize in unions in order to obtain and defend their rights through collective bargaining.

Moreover, workers' rights and duties as well as management's rights and duties are to be understood within the larger framework of the common good, a key principle of all social organization in Catholic social teaching. The common good stands as a corrective to the excessive individualism in United States society today. Simply stated, the common good is the "sum total of all those conditions of social living—economic, political, cultural—which make it possible for women and men readily and fully to achieve the perfection of their humanity. Individual rights are always experienced within the context of promotion of the common good."[2] It is the responsibility of government, business, mediating institutions such as labor unions and all citizens to promote, protect and be accountable to the common good of the community. Today, that community includes families, neighborhoods, cities, nation-states and the community of creation.

Women's Perspective

The issues of work and family are critical in a feminist reflection on Catholic social thought because today so many women find themselves caught between the demands of employment and family. For all too many women, particularly women heads of families, the double work day is the norm: They work all day at their place of employment and return home at night to do the work of family life and maintenance. Furthermore, women also suffer injustice in both these work places.

In examining Catholic social teaching documents, several key questions need to be considered: What is the image of family? Who is considered the worker? What is the image of work?

The image of family in the documents is the patriarchal family with very clear role delineations and authority structures. The ideal is the so-called "traditional family" with a father who is employed and a mother who takes care of the home and children. It was the image of the middle-class family that emerged with the Industrial Revolution, but it was never the universal experience of families. Poor and working class women have always had to work outside the home. Furthermore, this image does not reflect the reality of today's post-industrialized world. Nor is it an accurate representation of families in more traditional, pre-industrial or industrializing countries.

In the Church's concept of family, despite a few scattered references to women workers, the worker is male. Productive work is the work men do in the public arena. Women's work is confined to the home, and while its social value is recognized, there is no reflection on its economic value in the society. In Catholic social teaching, man is valued for his economic productivity and woman is valued for her social productivity.

Because the documents place so much stress on the meaning and role of motherhood, the meaning and role of fatherhood is insufficiently recognized. The purpose of raising these issues is not to deny or denigrate the social role and value of women who choose childrearing and homemaking as their primary work. Rather it is to bring into perspective the multiple roles and potential of women.

Moreover, to so emphasize that women are primarily responsible for the quality of family life diminishes the social role and value of fatherhood. It disenfranchises men from the full potential of their fatherhood while it disenfranchises women from the full potential of their personhood. Moreover, this division of labor is gender-based and does not take into consideration the individual woman or man's talents, gifts, education or desires.

Today, women remain primarily responsible for children and the quality of family life. Within most families there is an unequal distribution of labor between women and men. When the family life breaks down, women typically have custody of the children, often with insufficient or non-existent child support from the fathers. This reality, coupled with the inequities women commonly experience in the work place, has produced the phenomenon of the "feminization of poverty" in the United States.

The feminization of poverty, which should more accurately be called the "pauperization of women and children," raises the question of women's economic rights. Catholic social teaching has traditionally advocated the "family wage" as the way to guarantee economic

Because the documents place so much stress on the meaning and role of motherhood, the meaning and role of fatherhood is insufficiently recognized.

well-being for the family. But the "family wage" concept has been interpreted within the context of the so-called "traditional family." As such, it does not recognize the economic rights of a woman herself.

Today, on average in the United States, the full-time woman worker receives only $.69 for every $1.00 a man worker earns. If the female worker is African American or Hispanic, the wage differential is even greater. In this context, Catholic social teaching's insistence on just wages and benefits could assist women in the demand for justice in the work place.

The majority of women workers are concentrated in low-paying, low-benefit and dead-end jobs or are part-time or contingent workers with no benefits. More than three-fifths of those on minimum wage are women. Many women find themselves trapped in poor jobs for a variety of reasons, including gender and race discrimination, lack of affordable day care, limited training and educational opportunities, an education system in which school counselors and curriculum still subtly direct girls into traditional jobs and roles. The "traditional" cultural imperatives and expectations for women remain strong, despite a new economic and social reality that places new demands on and opportunities for women.

Women find themselves caught in conflicting messages and needs. Catholic education trains women for professions yet continues to hold out the ideal of the full-time mother. The Church encourages the laity to participate in the political processes, community service, schools and charity work to promote the common good. Women have always done the majority of volunteer work in this country. In addition, economic, social and personal needs move more and more women into the public sphere. These multiple demands of the family, the common good and the work place create stress, frustration and guilt in many women.

In reviewing how work and family are treated in the documents, our task is two-fold:

(1) To critique the documents in the light of contemporary experience, especially women's experience; and

(2) To offer ideas for a more adequate definition of work and family in the light of contemporary experience, especially women's experience.

---

[1] *Untitled,* Ecumenical Decade 1988-1998: Churches in Solidarity with Women: Prayers and Poems, Songs and Stories *(Geneva, Switzerland: World Council of Churches Publications, 1988), p. 64.*

[2] *Peter J. Henriot, Edward P. DeBerri, Michael J. Schultheis,* Catholic Social Teaching: Our Best Kept Secret, *rev. ed. (New York: Orbis Books, 1989), p. 21.*

The "traditional" cultural imperatives and expectations for women remain strong, despite a new economic and social reality that places new demands on and opportunities for women.

Catholic Social Teaching on Work and Family

THE CONDITION OF LABOR *(Rerum Novarum)* 1891:   It is a most sacred law of nature that the father of a family see that his offspring are provided with all the necessities of life and nature even prompts him to desire to provide and to furnish his children, who, in fact reflect and in a sense continue his person, with the means of decently protecting themselves against harsh fortune in the uncertainties of life. . . . As already noted, the family like the State is by the same token a society in the strictest sense of the term, and it is governed by its own proper authority, namely by that of the father [#20]. ◆ Finally, it is not right to demand of a woman or a child what a strong adult man is capable of doing or would be willing to do. . . . Certain occupations are less fitted for women, who are intended by nature for work of the home—work indeed which especially protects modesty in women and accords by nature with the education of children and the well-being of the family [#60].

THE RECONSTRUCTION OF THE SOCIAL ORDER *(Quadragesimo Anno)* 1931: In the first place, the worker must be paid a wage sufficient to support him and his family. . . . Mothers, concentrating on household duties, should work primarily in the home or in its immediate vicinity. . . . It is an intolerable abuse, and to be abolished at all cost, for mothers on account of the father's low wage to be forced to engage in gainful occupations outside the home to the neglect of their proper cares and duties, especially the training of children [#71].

PEACE ON EARTH *(Pacem in Terris)* 1963: Women have the right to working conditions in accordance with their requirements and their duties as wives and mothers. ◆ From the dignity of the human person there also arises the right to carry on economic activities according to the degree of responsibility of which one is capable. Furthermore—and this must be specially emphasized—there is the worker's right to a wage determined according to criteria of justice. This means, therefore, one sufficient, in proportion to the available resources, to give the worker and his family a standard of living in keeping with human dignity [#s 19-20].

ON HUMAN WORK *(Laborem Exercens)* 1981: Just remuneration for the work of an adult who is responsible for a family means remuneration which will suffice for establishing and properly maintaining a family and for providing security for its future. ◆ Experience confirms that there must be a social re-evaluation of the mother's role, of the toil connected with it and of the need that children have for care, love and affection in order that they may develop into responsible, morally and religiously mature and psychologically stable persons. It will redound to the credit of society to make it possible for a mother—without inhibiting her freedom, without psychological or practical discrimination, and without penalizing her as compared with other women—to devote herself to taking care of her children and educating them in accordance with their needs, which vary with age. Having to abandon these tasks in order to take up paid work outside the home is wrong from the point of view of the good of society and of the family when it contradicts or hinders these primary goals of the mission of the mother. ◆ The true advancement of women requires that labor should be structured in such a way that women do not have to pay for their advancement by abandoning what is specific to them and at the expense of the family, in which women as mothers have an irreplaceable role [#19].

Reflections

◆ What is the image of woman in these documents? Of man? Of the worker? Of work?

◆ Do these images respond to our contemporary experience in the United States?

◆ What effects has this image of woman and man had on family life? On the place of women and men in the public work place?

◆ Based on my experience, what is important? What is missing? What is inadequate?

◆ What are the difficulties women and men face today as they try to balance work, family and economic well-being?

Group Discussion:
Toward a Renewed Understanding of Work and Family

◆ What ideas need to be incorporated in Catholic social teaching to respond to contemporary reality more accurately?

◆ What new images of women, men and family need to be introduced into Catholic social teaching?

◆ How could Catholic social teaching approach the question of the equality of women and men in the home and in the work place more adequately?

TOWARD A RENEWED UNDERSTANDING OF THE HUMAN PERSON

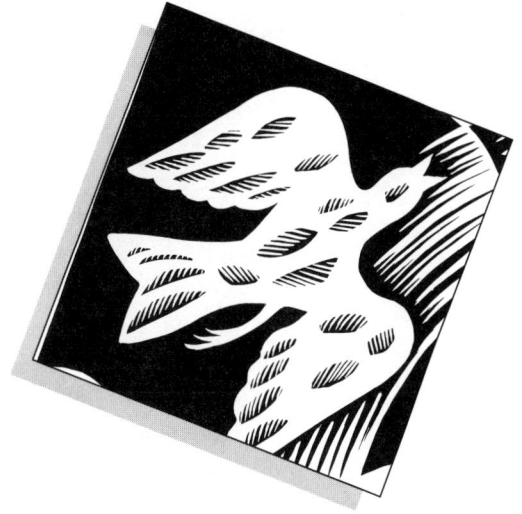

"Any human society, if it is to be well-ordered and
productive, must lay down as a foundation this principle, namely,
that every human being is a person, that is, his nature is endowed with
intelligence and free will. By virtue of this, he has rights and duties of his
own, flowing directly and simultaneously from his nature. These rights are
therefore universal, inviolable and inalienable.

Peace on Earth [#9]

"In Japan,
Once women were the sun.
Then women became the moon.
Now we women have started to restore
    our own self-esteem, our own self-dignity.
Yes, we women have started to realize
    the wholeness of humanity.
We women will do it
    with wisdom and the insights that we have been getting
    through our sensitivity to others' pains.
We women will do it
    with the power and the strength that we have been getting
    through our tenderness for others in need.
I trust women's sisterhood.
It's a big song, it's a big dream, it's a big spirit,
And it's a big path.

Satoko Yamaguchi,[1]
Japanese Poet

The dignity of the human person is the irreducible first principle of all Catholic social teaching. Every society, both religious and civil, is to be judged by the central question: Is the dignity of all human persons protected and enhanced by its laws and structures? Furthermore, the responsibility of the legitimate authority of all societies, both religious and civil, is to ensure that the rights of all citizens are guaranteed in order that the dignity of each person is protected and enhanced within a just social framework.

The Tradition

Peace on Earth is the Church's clearest declaration of human rights. In this encyclical, John XXIII enumerates the rights and consequent duties of every human person. These include political, economic, civil, legal as well as religious, cultural, educational rights and the right to choose one's own state of life. The duties demand that each citizen respect the rights of all others.

Moreover, in this encyclical, John XXIII recognizes that one of the signs of the times is the emerging consciousness of women: ". . . it is obvious to everyone that women are now taking a part in public life. . . . Since women are becoming ever more conscious of their human dignity, they will not tolerate being treated as inanimate objects or mere instruments, but claim both in domestic and in public life, the rights and duties that befit a human person" [#41]. This section explicitly recognizes

However, it is not until the Synod statement of 1971, *Justice in the World*, that the Church applies to itself the criteria of justice it demands of the civil society.

that women, by virtue of their humanity, have the same rights and duties as men.

However, it is not until the Synod statement of 1971, *Justice in the World*, that the Church applies to itself the criteria of justice it demands of the civil society: "Within the Church rights must be preserved. No one should be deprived of his ordinary rights because he is associated with the Church in one way or another. Those who serve the Church by their labor, including priests and religious, should receive a sufficient livelihood and enjoy that social security which is customary in their region. Lay people should be given fair wages and a system for promotion. . . .We also urge that women should have their own share of responsibility and participation in the community life of society and likewise of the Church" [#s41-42].

Women's Perspective

This principle of the dignity of the human person is significant in a feminist reflection on Catholic social thought for two reasons. First, it supports women's struggle for equal rights and opportunities in both the Church and in the society. And second, the Church's traditional understanding of the human person—its theological anthropology—needs to be re-examined in the light of the current historical shift in human consciousness regarding women.

Several difficulties are inherent in this examination. First, most English translations of the encyclicals use *man* or *mankind* as generic words for men and women. But the affirmations concerning man do not apply universally and equally to women and men, as the passages which specifically name women indicate. Some of the confusion rests in the problem of language, but a more serious confusion arises in the distinctions made between "human nature" and "woman's nature."

What do the documents intend when they speak of "women's proper nature" or when they limit women's world to that which is "according to her nature?" Are there two human natures—human nature, for which the male experience is normative, and then woman's nature?

As noted in the section on work and family, woman's capacity for childbearing is the critical issue. Whereas, women are identified and circumscribed by motherhood, men's identity is never limited by fatherhood. Is the documents' way of addressing this significant reality in most women's lives adequate as the universal criteria for the totality of all women's lives? What about women before and after childbearing? What about women who never bear children? To raise this question is not to deny the profound importance of sexuality—female and male—in the human experience and identity. It is to challenge that a woman is defined primarily by this single dimension.

Contemporary women's liberation struggle finds its power in the assertion of the full humanity of women. It rejects the concept of a dual human nature, pointing out that the very concept of "women's proper place" has been used to keep women in a subordinate position in all social and religious structures and to deny them access to the full exercise of their human rights. It rejects all personal attitudes, social systems, cultural mores or political and economic structures which explicitly or implicitly assume the natural superiority of men over women. It directly challenges the time-honored patriarchy that has shaped our world and our Church, from personal/familial systems to cultural/social structures.

Catholic social teaching's insistence on the dignity of the human person is a strong ally in women's struggle for equal rights, even though the Church itself is not yet able to recognize and guarantee those rights within its own life and structures. In fact, in the case of women, the Church stands judged by its own teaching.

While Catholic social teaching consistently affirms the dignity of the human person, the application of that teaching is shaped by its theological anthropology—its understanding of the human person. A close reading of the documents reveals that the Church uses different standards for women and men.

Moreover, the understanding of human nature is not static, but is constantly being formed and reformed by human experience shaped by historical, cultural, economic, political and social realities. The clearest example of this reformation of the Church's anthropological understandings is its changed attitude concerning slavery. For centuries, the Church not only justified the institution of slavery, but also owned slaves. It took the historical shift in human consciousness during the 19th century to move the Church to the

Contemporary women's liberation struggle finds its power in the assertion of the full humanity of women.

awareness that slavery is contrary to the dignity of the human person.

Today, the changing consciousness of women requires the Church to re-examine its assumptions about women, and therefore, about men. In the re-examination of Catholic social thought, several questions need to be addressed. How does Catholic social teaching understand the human person, especially the woman person? Does that understanding reflect contemporary women's experience? Which woman's experience is being reflected? How does Catholic social thought understand the man person? Does that understanding reflect contemporary men's experience? Which man's experience is being reflected?

In reviewing how women are treated in the documents our task is two-fold:

(1) To examine the theological anthropology in the context of experience, especially women's experience; and

(2) To offer a reformulated anthropology that more faithfully reflects contemporary human experience, especially women's experience.

---

[1] "Poem", The Best of Struggles: Multicultural Women's Project in Music, (Plainville, MA: Womancenter at Plainville, 1989), p. 17.

Catholic Social Teaching on
Women and Men

THE RECONSTRUCTION OF THE SOCIAL ORDER (*Quadragesimo Anno*) 1931:
But to abuse the years of childhood and the limited strength of women is grossly
wrong [#71].

PEACE ON EARTH (*Pacem in Terris*) 1963: Human beings have, in addition, the
right to choose freely the state of life which they prefer. They therefore have the
right to set up a family, with equal rights and duties for man and woman, and also
the right to follow a vocation to the priesthood and religious life [#15]. ◆ Secondly,
it is obvious to everyone that women are now taking a part in public life. This is
happening more rapidly perhaps in nations with a Christian tradition, and more
slowly, but broadly, among peoples who have inherited other traditions or
cultures. Since women are becoming ever more conscious of their human dignity,
they will not tolerate being treated as inanimate objects or mere instruments, but
claim both in domestic and in public life, the rights and duties that befit a human
person [#41].

THE CHURCH IN THE MODERN WORLD (*Gaudium et Spes*) 1965: Nevertheless,
with respect to the fundamental rights of the person, every type of discrimination,
whether social or cultural, whether based on sex, race, color, social condition,
language, or religion, is to be overcome and eradicated as contrary to God's intent
[#29]. ◆ As for the family, discord results from demographic, economic, and
social pressures, or from difficulties which arise between succeeding generations
or from new social relationships between men and women [#8] (from the section
Imbalances in the Modern World). ◆ In every group or nation, there is an ever-
increasing number of men and women who are conscious that they themselves
are the artisans and the authors of the culture of their community. . . .Women are
now employed in almost every area of life. It is appropriate that they should be
able to assume their full proper role in accordance with their own nature
[#s 55 and 60].

A CALL TO ACTION (*Octogesima Adveniens*) 1971: Similarly, in many countries a
charter for women which would put an end to an actual discrimination and
would establish relationships of equality in rights and of respect for their dignity is
the object of study and at times of lively demands. We do not have in mind that
false equality which would deny the distinctions laid down by the Creator himself
and which would be in contradiction with woman's proper role, which is of such
capital importance, at the heart of the family as well as within society. Development in legislation should on the contrary be directed to protecting her proper
vocation and at the same time recognizing her independence as a person, and her
equal rights to participate in cultural, economic, social and political life [#13].

JUSTICE IN THE WORLD 1971: We also urge that women should have their own share of responsibility and participation in the community life of society and likewise of the Church [#42].

ON HUMAN WORK (*Laborem Exercens*) 1981: Having to abandon these tasks (taking care of her children) in order to take up paid work outside the home is wrong from the point of view of the good of society and of the family when it contradicts or hinders these primary goals of the mission of the mother. ◆ The true advancement of women requires that labor should be structured in such a way that women do not have to pay for their advancement by abandoning what is specific to them and at the expense of the family, in which women as mothers have an irreplaceable role [#19].

Reflections

◆ How is woman understood in these documents? How is man understood?

◆ What do I agree with? Why? What do I disagree with? Why?

◆ How has this theological anthropology defined and limited women's roles in religious and social structures?

◆ Based on your experience, what is important? What is missing? What is inadequate?

Group Discussion:
Toward a New Anthropology

◆ What ideas would shape a theological anthropology that better responds to both women's and men's experience today?

◆ How could Catholic social teaching contribute to the understanding of both the distinctiveness and the radical equality of women and men?

◆ How would such a renewed anthropology begin to reshape religious and social institutions, particularly the Church, the work place and the home?

Toward a Culture of Peace

"Peace cannot be limited to a mere absence of war,
the result of an ever precarious balance of forces. No, peace
is something that is built up day after day, in the pursuit of an order
intended by God, which implies a more perfect form of justice among men.

The Development of Peoples [#76]

"I want a new Order!
To flood the world with laughter, songs, schools
bread, poems, children without hunger, young
people without war.

I want so much and am only a tiny untiring ant
laboriously carrying the painful grams of history.

I want so much and am only a woman
of tenderness, hungry,
a mountain blossoming
a waterfall
with a torrent of love
whirling inside. . .

Marianella Corriols Molina
Nicaraguan Poet[1]

Catholic social teaching is clear in recognizing that the fundamental dignity of the person and well being of the family is realized only in the context of a just and peaceful society.

World peace is a major concern in the more recent encyclicals. In these documents, the "just war" theory is addressed which outlines the criteria by which the morality of war can be evaluated. But they also challenge us to envision a peace that represents more than the absence of war. A new attitude towards war is recommended—one that has justice as its root.

The Tradition

Although Catholic social teaching focuses primarily on peace in relation to the just war theory, the encyclicals reflect a fairly constant suspicion that war has economic roots.

This broader approach to peace is seen in one of the major encyclicals on peace, John XXIIIs *Peace on Earth*. This document is known for its compendium of rights proper to each individual as well as for its emphasis on the economic roots of war.

John XXIII explains that the norms of truth and justice should regulate the relations between states. He discusses how states should work together for the common good. He sees that the arms race violates justice because it deprives individuals and nations of the resources they need to develop their own common good and jeopardizes the well-being of people by increasing the likelihood of war and by harming the environment in which people live.[2] In addition, John XXIII seriously challenges the morality of a nuclear war.

The advent of nuclear weapons radically challenged the traditional definitions of a just war. The Second Vatican Council in its document, *The Church in the Modern World*, addresses the issues of war and peace within this new reality. It is unequivocal in its condemnation of "any act of war aimed indiscriminately at the destruction of entire cities or extensive areas." It states that we need to approach the evaluation of war "with an entirely new attitude."

Paul VI continues exploring new dimensions of the traditional approach to war. In *The Development of Peoples,* he states that "development is the new name for peace." He clearly links economic justice and the use of resources with the definition of peace.

In *The Social Concerns of the Church*, John Paul II explores the connection between the arms race and imperialism. He argues that the arms race is not a form of national security but rather a threat to world peace. He contends that those who have the power of ultimate destruction may also be able to obtain the power to control the world.[3]

Catholic social teaching on war and peace has moved from very clear-cut definitions to more complex understandings that take into consideration the economic implications of war as well as the quest for power that legitimizes such domination. To develop "an entirely new attitude toward war" is still the challenge before us.

The arms race violates justice because it deprives individuals and nations of the resources they need to develop their own common good.

Women's Perspective

Women have been intimately bound up with war. We are not the decision-makers or conquerors but rather the conquered and the victims of the ravages of war.

It is our husbands, fathers, lovers, brothers, sons and daughters who are taken from us to fight the wars. Throughout history, we have been one of the spoils of war. Like the earth, women are violated in a war. Both are seen as territory that can be dominated, conquered and exploited.

Greed and domination are often the motivations for war. Such motives are legitimized and even celebrated in our political and economic structures. In a patriarchal culture, these motives are translated into a philosophy which sees both human and non-human relationships as paradigms of power and submission.[4]

Because most women have had to bear the domination-submission patterns of behavior on all levels, we bring a unique perspective to name the immoral consequences for societies which always prepare for war, engage in war, define their history through wars and define peace only as the absence of war.

Some women can also provide insights into what might constitute "an entirely new attitude toward war." Such an approach would go beyond the considerations of what constitutes a just war.

This new attitude would transform the very way we relate to each other at all levels—as woman/man, nation/nation and person/nature. It would challenge the quest for greed and power as a legitimate shaper of our institutions and structures. It would call into question the use of war as an acceptable means to settle conflicts and disputes. It would call for a conversion from a patriarchal mentality to one that understands power in new ways and believes in the equality of persons and the importance of mutual relationships.

What are some of the seeds of such a radical transformation? Studies in feminist psychology show that the way women have been socialized provides a set of values essential for the survival of humanity and the earth.

Women, for the most part, grow up within a patriarchal culture separated form the public arena where competition, aggression and domination are pursued and valued. Women are socialized in the more private arenas of life in which behaviors reflecting the values of cooperation, mutuality and interdependence are fostered. This socialization process strengthens our insights that relationships are key to our development as individuals and in community with all of creation. It provides the context of our own moral development which reveals an ethic of care and responsibility.

Many feminist theorists would concur with Mary Grey, that "these relational strengths—vital for all humanity—have been preserved, developed, but omitted from the transmission of official history" and that "interdependence and relating are the very threads of the complicated tapestry of the world."[5]

Many women seek mutuality in relationships. We seek to transform the oppressive domination/submission

> **B**ecause most women have had to bear the domination/submission patterns of behavior on all levels, we bring a unique perspective to name the immoral consequences for societies [of]...war.

patterns of relating on all levels. This feminist perspective could enhance the fuller development of "an entirely new attitude toward war"—even transform it into a new culture of peace.

Women's instinct that relationships are at the core of the universe have led us to work actively in the causes of peace, against the militarization of our culture, our economy and our foreign policy, and more recently, against environmental degradation. Many women have created ways of structuring relationships within the family to provide an opportunity for family meetings and deliberations on decisions that affect everyone. In the work arena, when women have the freedom to develop their own management styles, there is much emphasis on consensus and cooperation. Attempts are made to create structures that value the radical equality we all share as human persons as well as to appreciate our differences in skills and talent.

In reviewing how peace is addressed in the encyclicals our task is two-fold:

1) To critique the documents in light of what additional questions, insights, comments women's experience offers in addressing the definition of peace; and

2) To reflect on how women's experience points to ways of creating a whole new attitude toward war.

---

[1] "I Picture Sadness Sleeping," The Best of Struggles: Multicultural Women's Project in Music (Plainville, MA: Womancenter at Plainville, 1989), p. 26.

[2] Thomas A. Shannon, What are They Saying about Peace and War? (New York/Ramsey: Paulist Press, 1983), p. 26.

[3] Ibid, p. 30.

[4] Mary Grey, Feminism Redemption and the Christian Tradition, (Mystic, Connecticut: Twenty-Third Publications, 1990), p. 50.

[5] Ibid, p. 39. Ms. Grey further develops this point by showing how these studies are confirmed in systems theory and process thought which show the interrelatedness and interdependence of all the elements of the universe and makes relating a primary category of analysis. Pp. 40-46.

Catholic Social Teaching on Peace

PEACE ON EARTH *(Pacem in Terris)* (1963): On the other hand, it is with deep sorrow that we note the enormous stocks of armaments that have been and still are being made in the more economically developed countries with a vast outlay of intellectual and economic resources. And so it happens that, while the people of these countries are loaded with heavy burdens, other countries as a result are deprived of the collaboration they need in order to make economic and social progress [#109]. ◆ All must realize that there is no hope of putting an end to the building up of armaments, nor of reducing the present stocks, nor still less of abolishing them altogether, unless the process is complete and everyone sincerely co-operates to banish the fear and anxious expectation of war with which men are oppressed. If this is to come about, the fundamental principle on which our present peace depends must be replaced by another, which declares that the true and solid peace of nations can consist, not in equality of arms, but in mutual trust alone [#113]. ◆ There is reason to hope, however, that by meeting and negotiating men may come to discover better the bonds—deriving from the human nature which they have in common—that unite them, and that they may learn also that one of the most profound requirements of their common nature is this: That between them and their respective peoples it is not fear which should reign but love, a love which tends to express itself in a collaboration that is loyal, manifold in form and productive of many benefits [#129].

THE CHURCH IN THE MODERN WORLD *(Gaudium et Spes)* 1965: Peace is not merely the absence of war. Nor can it be reduced solely to the maintenance of a balance of power between enemies. Nor is it brought about by dictatorship. Instead it is rightly and appropriately called "an enterprise of justice" (Is.32:7) [#78]. ◆ If peace is to be established, the primary requisite is to eradicate the causes of dissension between men. Wars thrive on these, especially on injustice. Many of these causes stem from excessive economic inequalities and from excessive slowness in applying the needed remedies. Other causes spring from a quest for power and from contempt for personal rights. If we are looking for deeper explanations, we can find them in human jealousy, distrust, pride and other egotistic passions [#83].

THE SOCIAL CONCERNS OF THE CHURCH *(Sollicitudo Rei Socialis)* 1987: It was inevitable that by developing antagonistic systems and centers of power, each with its own forms of propaganda and indoctrination, the ideological opposition should evolve into a growing military opposition and give rise to two blocs of armed forces, each suspicious and fearful of the other's domination. ◆ International relations, in turn, could not fail to feel the effects of this "logic of blocs" and of the respective "spheres of influence." The tension between the two blocs which began at the end of the Second World War has dominated the whole of the subsequent forty years. Sometimes it has taken the form of "cold war," sometimes of "wars by proxy," through the manipulation of local conflicts, and sometimes it has kept people's minds in suspense and anguish by the threat of an open and total war. ◆ Although at the present time this danger seems to have receded, yet without completely disappearing, and even though an initial agreement has been reached on the destruction of one type of nuclear weapon, the existence and opposition of the blocs continue to be a real and worrying fact which still colors the world picture [#20]. ◆ It is this abnormal situation (the development of the East and West blocs), the result of a war and of an unacceptable exaggerated concern for security, which deadens the impulse towards united cooperation by all for the common good of the human race, to the detriment especially of peaceful peoples who are impeded from their rightful access to the goods meant for all. ◆ Seen in this way, the present division of the world is a direct obstacle to the real transformation of the conditions of underdevelopment in the developing and less advanced countries. However, peoples do not always resign themselves to their fate. Furthermore, the very needs of an economy stifled by military expenditure and by bureaucracy and intrinsic inefficiency now seem to favor processes which might mitigate the existing opposition and make it easier to begin a fruitful dialogue and genuine collaboration for peace [#22].

Reflections

◆ Reflecting on my experience as a woman or with women, what insights do I
bring to enhance the Church's teaching on peace?

◆ What has been my experience in working for peace in my family, community
and in society?

◆ What are the essential elements in creating "a new attitude towards war" or a
new culture of peace?

Group Discussion:
Toward a New Culture of Peace

◆ From our experience as women and with women, what are the essential elements of creating a "new culture of peace?"

◆ What changes in behavior would be necessary to create a new culture of peace in family, community, society and Church?

Toward an Understanding of Humane Economic Development and Organizing for Change

"True development, in keeping with the specific needs of the human being—man or woman, child, adult or old person—implies, especially for those who actively share in this process and are responsible for it, a lively awareness of the value of the rights of all and of each person. It likewise implies a lively awareness of the need to respect the rights of every individual to the full use of the benefits offered by science and technology.

The Social Concerns of the Church [#33]

"Women, . . . know that the women's struggle can only be won in the larger struggle. For a people cannot be free, until the women are free.

We want to add our strength and our vision to the movements that struggle for the right to live as human beings in freedom, dignity and equality.

Anonymous

Catholic social teaching clearly asserts that to achieve full human dignity it is critical that one's basic human needs are fulfilled. It is also clear that the fullness of human development is rooted in economic justice and world peace.

The Church judges various models of industrial economic development inadequate if they do not value the dignity and rights of persons. Changing how we approach development is a political as well as an economic task.

The Tradition

With the writing of *Christianity and Social Progress* in 1961, the Church recognized that social questions are world wide. The universal Church became global in its social concerns.

This dimension of global identity was strengthened during the Second Vatican Council. Prior to the council, the official teaching tended to be un-critical toward Western models of development. As Bishops from Africa, Asia, Latin America and Eastern European countries shared the suf-fering of their people and critiqued Western economic structures, a new awareness emerged.

The Church began to recognize that there is a plurality of economic models and that each country must find the one that best serves the welfare of its people. Breaking down the barrier of "West means best" represents a signifi-cant shift in the approach to interna-tional development.

Part of this shift, as expressed in *The Church in the Modern World*, is that the plight of the poor is a central concern.

The document states that the poor have a right to share in the fruits of the earth and a new economic order is one in which poor nations would have a more equal share of the world's goods and services.

In *The Development of Peoples*, Paul VI further elaborates this new approach to development. He sees development, the attainment of full self-development on the part of the poor of the world, as the new name for peace. He makes explicit reference to the harmful effects of multinational corporations' growing control of capital resources. He states that there is an increasing concentra-tion of wealth that must be addressed. This necessitates "bold transformations" of existing social structures. The trans-formations are to be carried out in a new spirit of global solidarity.

In *The Social Concerns of the Church*, written in honor of the 20th Anniver-sary of *The Development of Peoples*, John Paul II again addresses the themes of development, global solidarity and the need for structural change in light of contemporary realities. He denounces the increasing poverty which deprives millions of children, adults and elderly of the necessities of life and from hope that things could get better. This under-development which so many experience is assessed not only by the way goods and services are produced and distrib-uted but also by social and cultural indices—literacy, access to higher edu-cation, political participation, religious freedom, freedom from exploitation and all forms of discrimination.

John Paul II states that modern underdevelopment is not only an economic issue but also a cultural, political and human issue. This understanding of development leads him to conclude that the current models of economic development are too narrow in scope—at the core they value only economic realities and not the full development of the human person.

John Paul II critiques the current economic development models rooted in Western liberal capitalism and in Marxist collectivism. These underlying and opposing ideologies promote very different ways of organizing economic life, and they developed into antagonistic systems, creating centers of power which evolved into military opposition. Maintaining military strength and this division of power has polarized the world and posed direct obstacles to transforming the conditions of underdevelopment. Even though relations between the United States and the Soviet Union have begun to change, the effects of this 40-year bipolar division of the world continue to be felt as countries struggle to engage in economic development.

In addition to critiquing the dominant economic models, John Paul II also describes the moral obstacles to authentic human development. He names the "structures of sin" as the roots of the injustices confronting us. Two attitudes which contribute to the creation of such structures are "the thirst for power" and the "all-consuming desire for profit." To overcome these, he argues, individuals, nations and political blocs need conversion toward interdependence and "solidarity." He defines solidarity "as a firm and persevering determination to commit oneself to the common good; that is to say, to the good of all and of each individual because we are all really responsible for all" [#38].

The document calls upon us to question and analyze the structures of discrimination and exploitation. It also calls upon us to develop strategies to overcome the structures of sin in our historical reality.

In developing these strategies for change, the Church has raised up the importance of engaging in political activity. The Church affirms the responsibility of legitimate authority to guarantee the rights and duties of every citizen. At the same time, it realizes that in many instances the ability of a society to achieve justice is blocked by existing power structures. The Church recognizes the existence of unjust institutions—economic and political, cultural, military—which reinforce each other and are usually controlled by a small power elite which dominates a nation.

In *A Call to Action*, Paul VI states that the injustices within nations and within the international community have become so blatant that "many people are reaching the point of questioning the very model of society. . . . The need is felt to pass from economics to politics" [#45-46].

In *The Development of Peoples*, Paul VI addresses the issue of political engagement for both the official Church and the People of God. He calls for concerted political action to achieve the transformation of current economic structures through meaningful political change and broader participation in political

The poor have a right to share in the fruits of the earth and a new economic order is one in which poor nations would have a more equal share of the world's goods and services.

decision-making. This is an acknowledgement that political action is necessary to set limits to economic power. Political action is also needed at the global level to insure international cooperation and collaboration in order to transform economic structures.

The need for political action affirms the right of people and nations to participate in the decisions that affect their lives. This realization sensitizes the teaching Church to the importance of people organizing for change to achieve economic justice. It also sensitizes the Church to its own teachings on subsidiarity—the principle that those closest to a situation can best determine what is needed.

Women's Perspective

A key insight of Catholic social teaching that the dignity of the human person is at the center of any authentic model of development is confirmed in the experience of women who often bear a disproportionate burden of the failure of industrial models of development. In addition, women add the dimension of gender to the development question.

Agreeing with the Church's teaching, many women involved in development work understand that development is a political issue. As women organize to change and transform the oppressive structures, it becomes clear that those who suffer oppression must be central in planning and decision-making. This reality challenges women everywhere to deepen and broaden our understanding of feminism to include the struggles against sexism, racism, classism and excessive nationalism. The experience of many women who work together for change also provides a challenging insight into the kinds of radical transformations that might occur when there is real participation in decision-making.

ECONOMIC DEVELOPMENT AND GENDER: Women, especially women of color, are disproportionately the poor of our world. Women's experiences in developing countries offer a unique perspective in critiquing current economic models of development. The work undertaken by Development Alternatives with Women for a New Era (DAWN) is critical in any feminist analysis of development. DAWN is a network of women activists, researchers and policymakers committed to developing alternative frameworks and methods to attain the goals of economic and social justice, peace and development, free of all forms of oppression by gender, class, race and nation.

DAWN's book, *Development, Crises, and Alternative Vision*, states how most industrial models of development fail to achieve the basic human requirements needed for the majority of the world's population to survive. According to DAWN, "during the past decade, the majority of the world's population finds it increasingly difficult to fulfill even the basic requirements of life and to survive from one day to the next. Rather than channelling available resources into programs aimed at eliminating poverty and the burden of gender and other forms of subordination, nations and the international

The need for political action affirms the right of people and nations to participate in the decisions that affect their lives.

policy have tended to react to these pressures through increased militarization, domestic repression and foreign aggression."[2]

DAWN's analysis also raises gender as a key issue for development.

Conflicts arise between women's economic well-being and wider developmental plans and processes. They also occur because gender relations oppress women and because many long-term economic processes have been harmful or indifferent to the interests and needs of the poor. . .

Women's vulnerability is reinforced by systems of male domination that, on the one hand, deny or limit their access to economic resources and political participation, and on the other hand, impose sexual divisions of labor that allocate to them the most onerous, labor-intensive, poorly rewarded tasks inside and outside the home—and the longest working hours. . . . .In addition, gender-based subordination is deeply ingrained in the consciousness of both men and women and reinforced through religious beliefs, cultural practices and educational systems that assign to women lesser status and power.[3]

Any authentic model of development must recognize that in most countries "women's contributions—as workers and as managers of human welfare—are central to the ability of households, communities and nations to tackle the current crisis of survival."[4] Women bear the burden of survival which entails not only economic survival but the nurturing of culture, human relationships and community.

DAWN's vision of human economic development would transform poverty and gender subordination. It would eliminate inequality based on class, gender and race. The fulfillment of basic human needs would become basic rights and all forms of violence would be eliminated. Each person would have the opportunity to develop fully and women's values of nurturance and solidarity would characterize human relationships. Child care would be shared. Health care would be available as well as access to safe control of fertility. A nation's resources would be reordered from investment in military hardware to investment in people's basic needs. Institutions would foster participatory democratic processes and women would be involved in determining priorities and making decisions.[5]

ORGANIZING FOR CHANGE: Women understand that to achieve such a vision there must be political will. Because feminism is a political movement and a global one, there can be diversity in its issues and goals. As women continue to grow in their understanding that development is a political, economic and feminist issue, there is recognition that strategies for change must be developed with an openness and sensitivity to issues and methods as defined by different groups of women for themselves. "Acceptance of diverse feminisms does not deny the core commitment [of all feminisms]

As women organize to change and transform the oppressive structures, it becomes clear that those who suffer oppression must be central in planning and decision-making.

to eradicating the structures of gender subordination and achieving full and equal participation with men at all levels of society."[6]

This understanding enables us to link the struggles of sexism, racism, classism and nationalism. These linkages challenge both Catholic social teaching and our understanding of feminism. To achieve authentic human development poverty, racial and gender subordination must be transformed.

As women organize for change, many realize that to do it effectively demands the perspective of women who are the most oppressed. This belief has radical implications. The very processes by which strategies and development models are created must involve poor women. This reality challenges current structures and processes which reserve resources, power and control to small groups of people, usually men.

These same understandings, strategies and implications for action challenge not only the global women's movement but the feminist movement within each nation. Within the United States, women of color are leading the way in connecting the goals of eliminating racism, classism, nationalism and sexism. Together, women of color and white women are working to transform organizational structures of decision making which maintain unequal access to power based on race and ethnic origin. As women gain

access to decision-making structures, they examine and transform established rules, regulations, norms and operating assumptions and, where necessary, transform them to provide new relationships of power-power rooted in mutuality rather than in domination.

As women experience this new kind of power, their confidence increases. They bring these issues to other public arenas. Some women are engaging in political advocacy work on domestic and international issues. Some challenge forums from which they are excluded because of sex or race. Others are running for political office on platforms that advocate justice and peace.

Women are also challenging cultural and religious norms. Many women's religious congregations have transformed their hierarchical government structures into congregation-wide processes of participation. Many women are transforming marital relations into partnerships of mutuality and equality. As we gain confidence in the value of our experiences, we are willing to challenge decisions, decrees and norms that fail to incorporate our insights.

Once we understand and accept the diversity of feminism, we can then discover its power for change. It allows the struggle against domination to be waged in all arenas, from relations in the home to relations between nations.[7] For women, not only is the social question global but also, as the feminist movement has proclaimed, the personal questions are political. Relationships at all levels, personal,

Relationships at all levels, personal, professional, ecclesial and political, must reflect the same basic values of mutuality, participation and justice.

professional, ecclesial and political, must reflect the same basic values of mutuality, participation and justice.

In reviewing how economic development and political participation is handled in the encyclicals, our task is two-fold:

1) To critique the documents in light of what additional questions, insights, comments women's experiences offer in addressing questions of humane economic development and organizing for change; and

2) To reflect on how the principles, values and themes are already operative in some manner in women's lives.

---

[1] *Untitled*, Ecumenical Decade 1988-1998: Churches in Solidarity with Women: Prayers and Poems, Songs and Stories *(Geneva, Switzerland: World Council of Churches Publications, 1988), p. 64.*

[2] *Gita Sen and Caren Grown*, Development, Crises, and Alternative Visions, *(New York: Monthly Review, 1987), p. 16.*

[3] *Ibid., p. 16 and p. 26.*

[4] *Ibid., p. 18.*

[5] *Ibid., p. 80-81.*

[6] *Ibid., p. 79-80.*

[7] *Ibid., p. 19.*

Catholic Social Teaching on
Humane Economic Development and Political Participation

CHRISTIANITY AND SOCIAL PROGRESS (*Mater et Magistra*) 1961: From this it follows that the economic prosperity of any people is to be assessed not so much from the sum total of goods and wealth possessed as from the distribution of goods according to norms of justice, so that everyone in the community can develop and perfect himself. For this, after all, is the end toward which all economic activity of a community is by nature ordered [#74].

THE CHURCH IN THE MODERN WORLD (*Gaudium et Spes*) 1965: Every day interdependence tightens and spreads by degrees over the whole world. As a result the common good, that is, the sum of those conditions of social life which allow social groups and their individual members relatively thorough and ready access to their own fulfillment, today takes on an increasingly universal complexion and consequently involves rights and duties with respect to the whole human race. Every social group must take account of the needs and legitimate aspirations of other groups, and even of the general welfare of the entire human family [#26]. ◆ Praise is due to those national processes which allow the largest possible number of citizens to participate in public affairs with genuine freedom [#31]. ◆ Like other areas of social life, the economy of today is marked by man's increasing domination over nature, by closer and more intense relationships between citizens, groups and countries and their mutual dependence, and by the increased intervention of the state. At the same time progress in the methods of production and in the exchange of goods and services has made the economy an instrument capable of better meeting the intensified needs of the human family. ◆ Reasons for anxiety, however, are not lacking. Many people, especially in economically advanced areas, seem, as it were, to be ruled by economics, so that almost their entire personal and social life is permeated with a certain economic way of thinking. Such is true both of nations that favor a collective economy and of others. At the very time when the development of economic life could mitigate social inequalities (provided that it be guided and coordinated in a reasonable and human way), it is often made to embitter them; or, in some places, it even results in a decline of the social status of the underprivileged and in contempt for the poor. While an immense number of people still lack the absolute necessities of life, some, even in less advanced areas, live in luxury or squander wealth. Extravagance and wretchedness exist side by side. While a few enjoy very great power of choice, the majority are deprived of almost all possibility of acting on their own initiative and responsibility, and often subsist in living and working conditions unworthy of the human person [#63].

THE DEVELOPMENT OF PEOPLES (*Populorum Progressio*) 1967: For it is not simply a question of eliminating hunger and reducing poverty. It is not enough to combat destitution, urgent and necessary as this is. The point at issue is the establishment of a human society in which everyone, regardless of race, religion or nationality, can live a truly human life free from bondage imposed by men and the forces of nature not sufficiently mastered, a society in which freedom is not an empty word, and where Lazarus the poor man can sit at the same table as the rich man [#47].

A CALL TO ACTION (*Octogesima Adveniens*) 1971: The two aspirations, to equality and to participation, seek to promote a democratic type of society. . . .The Christian has the duty to take part in this search and in the organization and life of political society. As a social being, man builds his destiny within a series of particular groupings which demand, as their completion and as a necessary condition for their development, a vaster society, one of a universal character, the political society. All particular activity must be placed within that wider society, and thereby it takes on the dimension of the common good [#24].

THE SOCIAL CONCERNS OF THE CHURCH (*Sollicitudo Rei Socialis*) 1987: At the same time, in a world divided and beset by every type of conflict, the conviction is growing of a radical interdependence and consequently of the need for a solidarity which will take up interdependence and transfer it to the moral plane. Today perhaps more than in the past, people are realizing that they are linked together by a common destiny, which is to be constructed together, if catastrophe for all is to be avoided [#26]. ◆ Interdependence must be transformed into solidarity, based upon the principle that the goods of creation are meant for all. That which human industry produces through the processing of raw materials, with the contribution of work, must serve equally for the good of all. ◆ Solidarity helps us to see the "other"—whether a person, people or nation—not just as some kind of instrument, with a work capacity and physical strength to be exploited at low cost and then discarded when no longer useful, but as our "neighbor," a "helper," to be made a sharer, on a par with ourselves, in the banquet of life to which all are equally invited by God [#39].

Reflections

◆ Reflecting on my experience as a woman or with women, what insights do I bring to enhance the Church's teaching on humane economic development?

◆ As a citizen of the United States, what challenges do I face as I try to define models for authentic human development?

◆ As a citizen of the United States, what challenges do I face in being involved in political change?

◆ What blocks do I face in participating in the decisions that affect my life?

◆ What has been my experience in working to overcome the various forms of oppression in our society?

Group Discussion:
Toward an Understanding of
Humane Economic Development and Organizing for Change

◆ What insights do we have from Catholic social teaching as to what constitutes humane economic development?

◆ What insights can we draw from our experience as women and with women as to what constitutes humane economic development?

◆ What changes in behavior would be necessary for authentic models of development to exist in our society?

◆ What insight do we draw from Catholic social thought and our own experience on the importance of political change?

◆ What changes in behavior would be necessary if women were to have an equal voice in decision-making?

◆ What implications does such participation have for our family, community, society and Church?

Women as Church-in-action for Justice and Peace

"While the Church is bound to give witness to justice, she recognizes that anyone who ventures to speak to people about justice must first be just in their eyes. Hence we must undertake an examination of the modes of acting and of the possessions and life style found within the Church herself.

Justice in the World [#40]

"No! This, rather, is the fasting that I wish for you as women:
That you confront injustice in your communities, Church and world as a
  way of releasing those bound unjustly;
That you untie the thongs of patriarchy that have bound your bodies and
  your imaginations;
That you set free your own potential as women knowing that you cannot set
  free other oppressed persons unless you do;
That you work for breakthroughs in the yokes that prevent dialogue,
  reconciliation, and peacemaking. . . .

Then your light shall break like the dawn,
  and your woundedness as women shall quickly be healed.
Your vindication shall go before you,
  and my nurturing love will nourish you.

An adaptation of Isaiah 58
Barbara Valuckas, SSND[1]

For women who are Catholic and feminist, the personal is not only political, it is also deeply religious. By virtue of our baptism we are empowered and called to the mission of the Church, a mission of justice and peace for all.

The work for justice and peace, for social transformation, touches all dimensions of life. The feminist insight, "all is connected," reveals the integral nature of the human experience, and therefore, of justice and peace. It rejects the artificial dualism that separates the "private and the public sphere, production and reproduction, the household and the economy, the personal and the political, the realms of feeling and intuition and those of reason."[2]

Building on the work of *Christianity and Social Progress* and the Second Vatican Council, Paul VI, in *The Development of Peoples,* unequivocally states that "Today the principal fact we must all recognize is that the social question has become worldwide" [#3]. To this important truth, feminists add, it has also become personal and relational, not only in the relationships between women and men but also in the relationships between races, classes and nations. When these two truths are combined, the full task of the work for justice begins to be revealed and the vision of the reign of God is more fully realized.

The Synod document of 1971, *Justice in the World,* recognizes that the credibility of the Church's social teachings is determined by its ability to be just in its own life.

The Tradition

The Synod document of 1971, *Justice in the World,* recognizes that the credibility of the Church's social teachings is determined by its ability to be just in its own life. This reality creates a tremendous challenge to all of us as the People of God—women and men, laity, religious, clergy and hierarchy.

In recent years, with their pastorals on racism, peace, the economy and mission, the United States Bishops have been calling the U.S. Church to become more engaged in the mission for justice and peace. Their current pastoral-in-progress on women's concerns, despite its inherent problems, also reveals the Bishops' efforts to engage the Church in the critical issue of justice for women in our day.

In writing the pastorals on peace, the U.S. economy and women's concerns, the Bishops have initiated processes of wide consultation. These processes bring credibility to the pastorals by putting into practice some of the most important principles of Catholic social teaching, such as recognizing the dignity of the human person, support of the common good, participation, subsidiarity and linking the religious and social dimensions in peoples' lives. In fact, they have been an important breakthrough in understanding the role of the People of God in the Church's life and mission. Archbishop Rembert Weakland explains:

The model adopted by the U.S. conference believes that the Holy Spirit resides in all members of the Church and that the hierarchy must listen to what the Spirit is saying to the whole Church. This does not deny the teaching role of the hierarchy, but enhances it. It does not weaken the magisterium, but ultimately strengthens it. Discernment, not only innovation or self reliance, becomes a part of the teaching process."

Even when the Bishops have not always liked or agreed with what they heard—for example, in the consultations with women—the very process itself has demanded a mutual learning and listening that calls the whole Church to a mature reflection on and commitment to justice in its own life and structures while it calls the world to greater justice and peace.[3]

This integral commitment to justice is most clearly reflected in the pastoral on the economy, *Economic Justice For All: Catholic Social Teaching and the U.S. Economy*. After setting out the ethical norms by which to judge an economic system, critiquing the U.S. economy, identifying specific policy changes and calling for "A New American Experiment," the pastoral addresses the Church as an economic actor. In this section, five specific areas of economic justice for the Church to pursue are identified: wages and salaries, rights of employees, investments and property, works of charity and efforts toward economic justice.

Our Perspective

As we come to this last session, it is our belief that, as women, we have already begun to integrate into our lives and work many of the values and principles of Catholic social teaching. However, our experience leads us to raise critical questions when we encounter patriarchal biases or frameworks in Catholic social teaching.

Our experience of ourselves as women confirms the dignity and equality of women in all dimensions of life. We challenge outmoded concepts of work and family which have been developed without the participation of women who work both in the home and in the market place.

Our experience of violence toward women and children and of the militarism of our society and world increases our sensitivity to all forms of domination. We cherish a vision of peace for all, especially our loved ones. We work to provide a safe, secure and environmentally-sound world.

We are convinced by our experience that cooperation, participation and dialogue are key if we are to transform some of the unjust political, economic and social structures that maintain power and control over the majority of people in the world. We know that these patterns of relating must begin at home in family consultations, in relationships among siblings, in mutuality between marital partners. They must also be lived in the Church.

We have a deep suspicion about structures, organizations and attitudes that justify "the ways things are," blocking our ability to be engaged in informing, creating or enriching them.

And so, we, the authors of this book, believe that women are Church-in-action for justice and peace. Our experience is often unrecognized or unaffirmed. We need to articulate and celebrate our work for justice and peace. We know that as we share our

We are convinced by our experience that cooperation, participation and dialogue are key if we are to transform some of the unjust political economic and social structures.

wisdom, there is a beauty and truth in it. There is also pain. Our commitment to the Church and to its mission mandates us to denounce injustice wherever we find it—in society, in the world, but also in our Church and sometimes in our own families.

We also know that we cannot be about the liberation of others unless we recognize and struggle for our own liberation. Therefore, we call on our brothers in the Church, our colleagues in mission, our friends, lovers, husbands, sons and familial brothers to recognize that same truth in their own lives.

As we conclude our reflection on feminism and Catholic social teaching, we invite you to reflect upon your own life of justice and peace. How are you attempting to live the principles and values of Catholic social teaching and of feminism in all the dimensions of your life. What have you learned in the struggle?

Finally, let us recognize and affirm each other and our ongoing struggle to be Church-in-action for justice and peace. And let us not lose hope and energy as we live and sing the *Trouble and Beauty* of our commitment.

It's the star will rise and shine
rise and shine
It will rise and shine when earth's
people all are free
It calls to you, it calls to me
Keep your laboring wings
till all are free.

---

[1] *Printed in* Woman's Song *(Chicago: National Sisters' Vocation Conference, 1986), p. 55.*

[2] *Peggy Antrobus, "Gender Analysis," Unpublished manuscript, p. 24.*

[3] *"Where Does the Economic Pastoral Stand?" Origins, 13:46 (April 26, 1984), pp. 758-759.*

Reflections

◆ How have I and other women I know struggled to integrate the principles of Catholic social thought into the structures of

   ◆ Family?

   ◆ Work place?

   ◆ Religious communities?

   ◆ Church?

   ◆ Parish?

   ◆ U.S. society?

   ◆ World?

Group Discussion:
Toward a Renewed Commitment to Justice and Peace

◆ What are the examples of women as Church-in-action for justice and peace that we want to recognize and celebrate?

◆ What issues and new styles of relating do these examples suggest to assist the official Church in its desire to act for justice and peace?

◆ What new issues or actions has this process suggested to you as we begin the second century of Catholic social teaching?

C ENTER OF CONCERN

The Center of Concern is an independent, interdisciplinary team engaged in social analysis, theological reflection, policy advocacy and public education on issues of justice and peace. Rooted in a faith commitment and guided by a global vision, our current programs focus on international development, peace initiatives, economic alternatives, women in society and church, the cultural and ecological crisis and social theology. The Center holds consultative status with the United Nations. Our team engages in an extensive program of workshops and writing to help North Americans understand and respond to the changing global scene. A newsletter, *Center Focus*, is published bi-monthly. The Center is a tax exempt group and is supported largely by donations from friends.

Center of Concern
Resources in Catholic Social Thought

CATHOLIC SOCIAL TEACHING: OUR BEST KEPT SECRET

Peter Henriot, SJ, Ed DeBerri, SJ, Michael Schultheis, SJ

A helpful resource for studying the documents that have formed the Church's teachings on social issues. #4020 $7.95

OPTING FOR THE POOR: THE TASK FOR NORTH AMERICANS

Peter Henriot, SJ

Through accounts of personal experiences, the author clarifies who the poor are and presents compelling theological reasons, based on Scripture, why we as Christians must "stand with the poor" in their demand for justice. #4096 $5.95

SHAPING WELFARE CONSENSUS: U.S. CATHOLIC BISHOPS' CONTRIBUTION

Phil Land, SJ

A look at what's wrong and what's right in the present U.S. welfare system in light of the U.S. Bishops' Economic Pastoral. Offers a comprehensive examination of the current welfare debate from the perspective of Catholic social thought, with new emphasis on economic democracy and local participation. #4092 $7.95

Other Books by Maria Riley

WISDOM SEEKS HER WAY: LIBERATING THE POWER OF WOMEN'S SPIRITUALITY

Through a process of personal reflection and sharing, this beautiful book invites women to affirm the spirituality resulting from their unique experiences as women. #4075 $5.95

WOMEN FAITHFUL FOR THE FUTURE

A series of discussions designed for reflection on the implications of women's fidelity, women's experience and women's role in the future of society and the Church. #4060 $2.95

TRANSFORMING FEMINISM

A timely analysis offering a feminist critique of Catholic social thought and calling for a dialogue through which both feminism and Catholic social thought can be transformed. #4095 $8.95

To order these resources or to receive the *Center Focus* newsletter, please send your request to: Center Resources, 3700 13th Street, N.E., Washington, D.C. 20017 (202) 635-2757/FAX (202) 832-9494

◆ Add 15% for shipping and handling (minimum charge $1.00)

◆ A comprehensive Center Resource Catalogue is offered upon request.

LCWR
✝

Leadership Conference of Women Religious

The Leadership Conference of Women Religious is a national organization of approximately 800 women religious who are the principal administrators of their congregations. The purpose of the Conference is, "to promote a developing understanding and living of religious life through: 1) assisting its members, personally and communally to carry out their services of leadership; 2) fostering dialogue and collaboration among religious congregations within Church and society; and 3) developing models for initiating and strengthening relationships with groups concerned with the needs of society."

The goals of LCWR for 1989-1994 are:

1. To promote for ourselves and others modes of leadership consonant with our experience as women.

2. To articulate development in the contemporary theology of religious life in the context of the mission of Jesus and of our experience as U.S. women in the Church.

3. To collaborate with others in modes of interdependence and mutuality to shape a future based on Gospel values for Church and society.

4. To develop structures of solidarity with women in order to work for the liberation of women through the transformation of social and ecclesial structures and relationships.

5. To effect action for justice leading to systemic change locally and globally in order to bring about harmony among people in communion with the earth.

6. To work to eliminate the sin of racism in ourselves, our congregations, our institutions and in the other structures of Church and society.

CLAIMING OUR TRUTH: REFLECTING ON IDENTITY BY U.S. WOMEN RELIGIOUS
ed. Nadine Foley, OP

Probes the influences which have shaped renewal and the changing realities in religious congregations. 200 pp. $10.95

IMAGING GOD/WOMEN'S EXPERIENCE
intro, Joan Chittister, OSB

Analysis/reflection on women's experience of the Holy with group process design.
60 pp. $5.95

To place order, write:
LCWR
8808 Cameron Street
Silver Spring, MD 20910

NETWORK,

A National Catholic Social Justice Lobby

Since 1971, NETWORK has been lobbying Congress to enact laws providing economic justice for the poor, protecting human rights at home and abroad, promoting disarmament and insuring world peace.

Today, nearly 9,000 NETWORK members are united as women and men who put their faith into action by advocating for justice in legislation—for public policy that addresses the systemic causes of poverty and injustice.

Over the years, we have raised our voice successfully in Congress and have helped win legislation to: create the Consumer Cooperative Bank; curb spending on Star Wars; win ratification of the INF Treaty; stem the production of chemical weapons; win passage of the Voting Rights and Civil Rights acts; defeat military aid to the contras; impose sanctions on South Africa.

NETWORK Issue Agenda:

JUST ACCESS TO ECONOMIC RESOURCES
Housing ◆ Health ◆ Employment ◆ Income Support

FAIRNESS IN NATIONAL FUNDING
Military Spending Cuts/Economic Conversion ◆ Fair Taxation ◆ Deficit Reduction ◆ Human Needs Increases

JUSTICE IN GLOBAL RELATIONSHIPS
The Philippines ◆ Central America ◆ South Africa

As a member of NETWORK, you will send our lobbyists to Capitol Hill to voice your clear message on behalf of social justice. When you join NETWORK, you will receive timely information from our bi-monthly publication, *NETWORK Connection*, Actions Alerts, Phone Alerts, and Voting Records.

Send $30 annual membership fee to NETWORK, 806 Rhode Island Avenue NE, Washington, DC 20018, (202) 526-4070.

NETWORK Resources...

help you continue your reflection on Catholic social justice teaching and feminism:

SOCIAL JUSTICE ENCYCLICAL CHART:
Popular study chart of the Catholic Church's social encyclicals/documents. Includes articles by Maureen Aggeler, RSCJ, Carol Coston, OP, Amata Miller, IHM, Nancy Sylvester, IHM, study chart, questions for reflection and discussion.   1-5 copies $2.00 each

RELIVING OUR ROOTS:
Reflection/discussion process helps us clarify what it means to be a Catholic in our U.S. democracy. Excellent education resource when used with the Encyclical Chart.   1-5 copies $3.50 each
(when ordered with Chart: $3.00 each)

FEMINISM: VALUES AND VISION:
Booklet by Carol Coston, OP, offers a working definition of feminism, cites examples of feminist values, formulates an understanding of feminist values— "the first step toward transforming our world."   1-5 copies $3.00

Order from NETWORK, Box T-B, 806 Rhode Island Avenue NE, Washington, D.C. 20018. (202) 526-4070. FAX: (202) 832-4635. Bulk prices available.